THE POLITICS OF BIG DATA

THE POLITICS OF BIG DATA

Max Everest-Phillips

The Global Centre for Public Service Excellence

Singapore

Contents

Acknowledgments

As the Director of the Global Centre for Public Service Excellence, I was commissioned to write this discussion paper by the UN Global Pulse, Jakarta. I am grateful to the director of Global Pulse, Derval Usher, and policy specialist George Hodge, for their inspiring enthusiasm. Stuart Smith of the Institute of Systems Science, NUS kindly reviewed an early draft of the paper. Balázs Horváth, Director of UNDP's Seoul Policy Centre, offered valuable feedback.

A Note on 'Data'

'Data' is the plural of 'datum,' the Latin word for a piece of information. The term has been adopted into the English language. Not wishing to seem poorly educated, some authors, therefore, treat 'data' as a collective plural, and insist on writing "these data are" (like 'people': "the people <u>are</u> dissatisfied with this book" not "the people <u>is</u> dissatisfied with this book"). In colloquial and spoken English, 'data' is invariably used as a collective singular, like 'information' ("the information is good," not "the information are good"). In the democratic spirit honoured herein, the will of the people to ignore any pretension to a classical education is upheld: therefore "data is ..."

But don't worry: except for this note, the booklet you are about to read eschews pomposity and pedantry. If these traits have inadvertently slipped in, the author (an argumentative advocate for advertent alliteration) abjectly apologies in advance.

Summary: Key Messages

This discussion paper outlines the political dimensions of big data – and the big data aspects of politics. The topic is one of the looming but as yet poorly understood challenges facing humanity from the '4th Industrial Revolution', the ongoing digital transformation of society, the economy and politics through emerging technologies that include robotics, artificial intelligence, and The Internet of Things.

This booklet seeks to provide the reader with a perspective on how politics and big data are, will and can interact with each other, by placing current enthusiasms and anxieties about big data's potential in broad historical context. Big data will shift the political landscape. The public, civil society, firms, politicians and bureaucrats will increasingly seek to change the political landscape in the face of proliferating and deepening usage of big data. Big data is considered along with closely associated technologies, such as 'algorithmic decision making' (that is, accepting recommendations derived from machine learning algorithms that process the big data), that shape its applications.

Politics is the process of action and ideas to shape, gain and contend power. The politics of big data is concerned with the power relations over data, its collection, analysis and use. The state, citizens, civil society, and business all have interests and incentives to gather use, control, influence and subvert big data.

Big data is fundamentally different in scale and detail from traditional sources of knowledge. By changing the information on which policy choices are framed and resolved, it will affect, and be affected by politics. By offering unprecedented opportunities and challenges to the ways citizens and governments interact, it will alter the nature of the state and the nature of government. Big data politics will therefore have the potential to reconfigure the power dynamics of elites and shift the social contract between citizen and state.

All data that can form the basis for framing problems and suggesting solutions, is potentially political, for good or ill. No data is apolitical. Rather, its collection, analysis and use all depend on decisions made to collect, analyse and deploy that data. By the manner in which this process is managed, politics will refashion big data and transform the uses of evidence in government and society. Discrepancies *within the state* may grow if minorities are not included in big data, and *between* states in capacity of data collection/analysis. National capacity in big data will affect international competitiveness.

In the public sector, big data will transform the design, the delivery and the monitoring of public policies. It will dramatically transform public services into better targeted, needs-based delivery. That will increase the accessibility, reach and effectiveness of public services. By delivering to citizens the precise services that they need, big data can significantly improve public trust in political leadership. The result will be to boost the legitimacy of the state.

Big data will throw up new challenges requiring political judgment. Rapid and pervasive technological progress, including big data and the artificial intelligence (AI) that is derived from it, will have many disruptive effects, on labour markets, the economy and society, as well as in government. Managing these 'disruptions' will require political skill.

The politics of big data will also be affected by the private sector. Big business ownership of big data will strengthen the capacity of major international corporations to view, understand and potentially, in 'Big Brother' fashion, manipulate society for private gain. How the power derived from big data of giant conglomerates, the 'robber barons' of the 21st century, can be adequately contained will challenge governments everywhere. Public concerns over that unaccountable power, individual rights to privacy and unaccountable mass surveillance will create the biggest fault-lines in the politics around big data.

Another issue of political contestation will be the extent to which the past (data) can condemn the present and future, through its use by AI. As a result, the balance between privacy and the common interest will become more complex. One emerging example is the growing difference between the EU's and the US's approaches to regulating AI. EU rules create a right to explanation and a right to human review for automated decisions. These rules risk severely curtailing the use of AI, and the associated opportunities for productivity gains. The US currently prioritises sector-specific policies over comprehensive regulation in this field, emphasising the potential benefits of economic transformation over individual rights.

As the rights and liberties of the individual become more constrained, the limitations, errors and biases in data gathering and its interpretation will pose new problems and significant political challenges. The politics of data resistance and 'post-Truth' manipulation of public opinion and the electorate will increase the pressure on organizations to transform their practices and principles, including with regard to transparency and accountability. The extent to which the state should regulate in the interests of the subjects of the data, the data generators, or the data owners will become a further topic of political contention, not least "who will guard the guards?"

Another related concern will be the extent to which big data strengthens centralised control by being extracted for decision-making, or is locally-owned and emphasises the well-being of subjects of data such that they benefit most from the insights. This political contestation will confront the problem of 'legibility': the more data is collected, the more significant become the overt or hidden assumptions underlying its collection. Who chooses what data to collect or not, with what inherent bias in the underlying assumptions, will pose significant political challenges.

But, for all its potential, big data is fundamentally the same politically as traditional sources of knowledge in being subject to bias, hidden values and implicit assumptions. Many problems are about political values and not susceptible to solution by data, big or small or none at all. Indeed big data risks creating the delusion of a 'technocratic heaven.' This is the danger of falling into the trap of believing that, with the 'right' information, all problems have 'rational' best solutions without the need to resort to political choices, judgment and values.

The long view of history suggests that the biggest political challenge will be to ensure big data works for all, and is perceived as doing so. Overt political oversight will be needed if Governments are to demonstrate ethical collection, analysis and use of big data to maintain citizens' trust, and bolster the legitimacy of the state. Political unrest will result if big data and AI appear increasingly to be exacerbating discrimination, exclusion, or extreme inequalities.[1]

Big data, therefore, will further increase the need for effective institutions, magnify the impact of differences in the quality of government around the world and at sub-national level, and increase the need for effective politics that can strengthen the legitimacy of their governments and build citizen trust. Understanding and engaging with the politics of big data will prove to be an essential skill for public officials everywhere, including in seeking to deliver on the Sustainable Development Goals.

Chapter 1: Big Data and the State

"If a man will begin with certainties, he shall end in doubts; but if he will be content to begin with doubts, he shall end in certainties."

Francis Bacon (1605).
The Advancement of Learning, Book 1, v,8.

Introduction

The term "Big Data" refers to quantities of information so large and complex that traditional data-gathering cannot compete and traditional methods of data-processing cannot cope.[2] Big data is a product of increasingly cheap but disruptive technologies, including information-sensing mobile devices, aerial and other remote sensors, software logs, cameras, microphones, radio-frequency identification readers, and wireless sensor networks.[3]

In common usage, 'big data' refers to **quantity,** when data is too large to be stored locally and analysed by standard computers and software. But size is not the only defining characteristic, of whatever order of magnitude. In addition to volume, variety and velocity matter. Big data, however, is also unstructured or in multiple formats that are generated at speed and constantly changing. Big data is potentially revolutionary if it challenges the accepted understanding of the world. The dynamic **qualitative** nature of big data also matters, including data standards. Data, in other words, resembles crude oil: unrefined, neither can be used. Crude oil has to be changed into gas, plastic, chemicals, and so forth. Equally 'raw' data must be processed to a fixed or minimum quality to be useable for analysis. So big data (sometimes described as the 'oil of the 21st century,' for its potential economic importance) does not exist in some 'pure' or prelapsarian state of nature, untouched by human hand. Rather, data is mediated by the mechanisms, concepts, methods, platforms, scientific instruments, and so forth that generate them, and then shaped by the way that data are harvested, stored, analysed and visualized.

This applies to all data, but is all the more the case for big data, both in government and the private sector. For example, global web organisations are creating big data by synergising ever more services in search, map, data storage, data treatment, trade, and so forth. Such increasing visibility creates data credibility, while this big data-driven commercial power dynamics using quantitative methods are quickly but quietly transforming political processes and administrative decisions in everyday life. Political concepts are also continually reconfigured in response to shifting ideals, conceptions and practices of governance and democracy in different contexts.

The concept loosely describes the volume, velocity and variety of data, creating the phenomenon of rapidly increasing data generation (90% in the last two years), gathering and mining along with the various steps therein. These processes include data capture, curation, search, analysis, sharing, storage, transfer, and visualization – that are rapidly pervading every aspect of work in both the public and private sectors around the world. All these developments involve the capacity to collect, search, aggregate and cross-reference large data sets – be it in text, image, numeric or video formats - on an unprecedented scale.[4]

Big data's collection and analysis offers unparalleled and potentially revolutionary opportunities to improve the ways citizens and governments interact. Big data analytics and visualisation generate more and clearer information that strengthen service delivery, improve policies, inspire collective action and citizen feedback, prompting action and motivate political causes. 'What gets measured get done.'

The collection and analysis of 'big data' offers unprecedented revolutionary opportunities to improve the ways citizens and governments interact, but also present new challenges in the limitations, errors and biases in its gathering and interpretation.

For some time, the topics of big data and the consequent 'Data Revolution' [5] has been fashionable in politics – the UN, the White House and the European Parliament all released reports in 2014-15. [6] The Obama presidential campaign in 2008 and the 'Arab Spring' of 2011 first drew widespread attention to the political potential of new technologies, particularly social media. But, beyond concern for data security and privacy, the full extent of the potential political implications of big data for the governance context everywhere is only now starting to attract attention.

It is, however, already apparent that the big data revolution will affect and be affected by politics. The consequences will impact not just on operational efficiency of the delivery of public services and the accuracy of strategic planning and policy-making, but on relations generally between citizens and the state, and between politicians and public officials. Central and local governments round the world are already both creating and using big data for developing policy, planning and projects. Not surprising then that, in recent years, the distinct but associated concepts of big data and open data have been developing a central role in government policy and promoting the legitimacy of policy formulation.

The result is that big data has already produced impressive improvements. In Istanbul, for example, the mobile phone company Vodafone has deployed its huge database tracking where travel patterns enable a redesign of the city's entire bus route network to fit current needs rather than long-established but often redundant service routes. Dublin City Council provides near-real-time estimates for bus arrival and transit times using predictive analytics; while Los Angeles uses big data from magnetic road sensors and traffic cameras to control 4,500 traffic lights and thus the flow of traffic around the city, reducing traffic congestion by an estimated 16 percent. [7] Incentives are compelling.

BOX 1: How Big is 'Big Data'?

While quantity is not everything in big data, the numbers are indeed sizeable. In 2015, there were 2.6 billion email users worldwide with 4.35 billion email accounts sending 205 billion emails (including 12 billion spam) on average every day, or 75,000,000,000,000 in a year. By 2015, 61.2 percent of the world's population were using a mobile phone, and the global mobile wireless penetration stood at 94%, or 6.915 billion subscriptions (up from 5.86 billion in 2011). In China, the penetration rate of smartphone search users reached 88.3%, or 590 million people, and an astonishing 745 billion text messages were sent in that one country alone during the course of 2015. In the first six months of the year, over 8 million tweets worldwide were sent just on the topic of honest and responsive government, and a further 4.75million on political freedom.

The world's capacity to store information has roughly doubled every three and a half years since the 1980s. The emergence of cloud computing has led to new software and analytical tools to process vast quantities of data in near-real time. Already by 2012 (the last date about which there is general consensus over the figures), Facebook had 1 billion members (and, by 2015, it had 936 million users or an eighth of humanity logging in every day, up from 665m at the start of 2013), a Google search was examining 1.2 billion websites, and 2.5 exabytes (1 exabyte = 1,000,000,000,000,000,000, or a quintillion) of data were being created every day. It was then estimated that already over 90% of all data in existence had been generated and collected in just the previous two years.

In 2013, 4 zettabytes (1 zettabyte = 1,000,000,000,000,000,000,000 bytes, or a thousand exabytes) of data was generated worldwide, or the equivalent of 1292 trillion copies of Tolstoy's epic novel 'War and Peace'.[8] The US public sector stored 1.3 petabytes of data bn. in 2011. There is every reason to assume that this rate of data accumulation has continued growing apace and that it will persist into the foreseeable future.[9]

But today's big data may not seem so big as data analysis and computing technology relentlessly improve. Enthusiasm should also be tempered by the practical problem that, by some estimates, over 90 per cent of big data will never have any conceivable likely research use.[10]

The Politics of Data: who collects it for what purpose?

These developments will be revolutionary where on-line exchange platforms, such as social networks and social media, are also reframing the way citizens, businesses and political organisations present their thinking, mobilise and protest.[11] Big data as the result of new technologies creates increasingly sophisticated techniques for deepening democratic consultation, accountability and transparency. Government openness about data makes big data more useful, more democratic, and less threatening.

Traditionally, bureaucracies generated one-dimensional data. That product, although offering only a narrow map of reality, served its purpose – often the need to address fiscal pressures. By contrast, big data is more complex and fluid. These characteristics are new and the implications still uncertain, but have the potential to offer more 'three-dimensional' policy. If so, the politics of big data differs from that of 'traditional' knowledge – and this may ultimately affect the political economy. Specifically, much of the data is currently owned by a few tech firms as a *commodity* rather than collected as crucial input for informed policymaking. This affects politically how people perceive big data, as enhancing user/consumer experience but contributing to suspicion of it, leading to a deficit in trust of big data. This can be tackled where political leaders encourage open data to make big data more effective and transparent. Political commitment to prevent big data from worsening inequalities and ensure fair access to its gains, while using it to expose corruption, would further boost trust between the public and the government.

More data, of course, does not of its own accord lead to progress. Information is a social construct. 'Campbell's law' suggests that the more a quantitative social indicator is used for social decision-making, the more it will distort and corrupt the social processes it is intended to monitor. [12] There is nothing inherently 'democratic' either about data or technology, or a combination of their use. In an era of big data, the tensions between liberty and the common good will become ever more apparent. Big data raises political issues concerning data protection, de-identification and privacy, transparency, citizenship, surveillance and the reshaping of the economy. It can risk becoming too closely associated with a particular government, political party or politician.[13]

Equally it has the potential to facilitate repressive control and authoritarian governance, including by fabricating political consent, sabotaging dissidence, cowering or co-opting civil society, threatening activists, and gathering personal data without citizens' agreement. [14] Big data will empower dictatorships by enabling increasingly sophisticated techniques of control and repression. It will be used for fabricating political consent, sabotaging peaceful protest, destabilizing dissidence, cowering or co-opting civil society, threatening activists, and gathering personal data without citizens' agreement.

But even in democratic polities, political problems will remain. Big data is exacerbating growing inequality. It can be misused and abused. There are limitations, errors and biases in its gathering and interpretation. Data privacy can be violated.

Government is data, as data shapes information that formulates policy and crafts the political narrative. Furthermore, big data is part of the ICT that appears to be changing people: human attention span has declined from 12 seconds in 2000 to 8 seconds in 2015, supposedly 1 second less than a goldfish, according to research by Microsoft Canada (but no time for further details).[15] By 2016, over half of the populations of the UK and the USA were regularly using Facebook. The UK's Brexit referendum and the US Presidential election that year suggest that these developments create an 'echo-chamber' of 'post-Truth' politics and 'policy making by Twitter', putting at risk citizens' capacity to appreciate complexity and find common ground.

In this new political context of the 'chaotic pluralism', "before the Internet becomes too ubiquitous, researchers and policy makers need to seize the current movement to understand the profound political changes already underway."[16] Big data analytics seems to be interacting with social-networking in making human attention span shorter, contributing to political echo-chambers.

More hopefully, big data may prove to be a political trigger for more effective, efficient, professional, and merit-based public service institutions able to restore citizens' trust. Widespread collaboration may form part of that shift. Citizens' access to big data can change the relationship between state and citizens, with crowdsourcing bypassing the public service's traditional monopoly on policy formulation. Big data in the hands of citizens is another potential for the democratisation of power, one that could radically shift political leverage.

Big data may also expose further the weaknesses of the state and society. Big data sources and technologies, however, must be applied carefully to avoid a reporting bias favouring more advantaged people and thus widening the gap between the "data poor" and the "data rich". The balance between privacy and the common interest will become more complex. Data that is not collected will reflect political options. The body of data collected and used for different purposes and agendas shapes the concentration of power.

A real data revolution can only take place if there exists strong political will to act upon the knowledge imparted by the data. In a 'post-truth,' 'alternative fact' world, big data offers the potential to transform political processes and decisions at the local, national and international level. Delivering better results may assist in reinforcing trust in government. Legal frameworks underpin visibility and credibility. Online exchange platforms, such as social networks and social media reframe the way citizens and political organisations engage, mobilise and protest.

Open data in text, image, numeric and video formats in unprecedented scales is widely available, while private companies and governments are developing uses of big data with major consequences for politics affecting relations between citizens and the state, the foundation of political legitimacy. The idea of the "end of politics" is tempting but idealistic; big data will have profound effects on impartial, equitable and meritocratic policymaking but cannot completely discard natural human systems directed by political leadership. The significant socio-economic advantages of big data are only possible if the institutions employing this new body of knowledge are effective, impartial and place importance on citizen welfare.

Furthermore, data is inherently political because its collection and use has the potential to affect power in different forms. This is most apparent as the authority of governing through public administration and expert power derived from control of data, the power derived from analysis of data to direct others and to deliver by resource allocation, but also the power informed by data of citizens in collective action, in a sense of rights, self-confidence and empowerment. Performance data drives funding, population data determines public service provision, and crime data directs policing. The nature of the information available, of course, always defines the problems governments face and shapes the solutions that public service administers. By helping to create effective institutions, effective databases like censuses or tax registries (like the Domesday Book of 1086, or the US Census of 1880) have always played a key role in the development of statehood and 'national' identities, and understanding of economic and social dynamics. Data generation creates politicised categorisation that can be designed to assist, control, coerce or even oppress: the poor, the unmarried mother, the illegitimate child, the ethnic minority, the unemployed, the disabled, or the elderly. There is nothing inherently democratic or developmental in digital communication technologies.

Pattern of big data business/government connections in Korea. Since the Open Data Law in 2013, there has been a massive increase in the datasets opened up by government: inter-active version at http://www.opendata500.com/kr/

Whatever the politics in any country around transparency, the politics of big data everywhere seems likely to result in significant political change affecting power relations between all the key stakeholders – leaders, public officials, citizens, private sector and civil society. Exactly what form this change will take is still unclear but the general trends are emerging. The nature of the governance context will shape the political credibility for the collection and use of big data in politically acceptable ways, constrain its abuse, and overcome entrenched divisions and practices of government.

BOX 2: How will Big Data change the nature of Government?

Big data and crowd-sourcing are examples of data innovation. Big data can help to foster 'whole of government' collaboration (the Prime Minister's Office in India is using big data techniques to turn ideas generated on its crowd-sourcing platform *mygov.in* into actionable reports for ministries to implement), create real-time solutions (crowd-sourcing information on potholes can cut repair costs and time), and usher in a new era in which citizens genuinely play an active role in the policy process (e.g.. USAID has used crowdsourcing to clean and geocode a dataset to open and map its data).

Big data can be exploited to filter out 'noise', in order to predict future behaviours and events with far greater accuracy than was possible in the past, while enabling more robust statistical analysis using such tools as Linear Regression, K-Factor, or Probability modelling, to identify trends that would otherwise be more difficult to observe.

This is already helping to improve governments' operational efficiency and, therefore, producing lower costs and reduced risk. For example, the *Bundesagentur für Arbeit* (Germany's Federal Labour Agency) analysis of its big data on interventions for unemployed workers led to reduced spending by €10 billion annually while cutting the amount of time that the unemployed took to find jobs, and increasing the satisfaction among users of its services.

In another example, the Los Angeles and Santa Cruz police departments have taken an algorithm used to predict earthquakes and used it with crime data. The result is software that can predict where crimes are likely to occur resulting in a 33% reduction in burglaries and 21% fall in violent crimes in areas where the system is being used.

In Beijing, big data is helping to predict air pollution 72 hours in advance— a promising tool for an environmental issue that, by one estimate, results in 1,000,000 deaths a year in China. Open Data Census provides data-transparency metrics, including in transportation, pollution and health performance. *Socrata*, *Hadoop* and *Alooma* can help governments and policymakers get new data initiatives off the ground by providing the infrastructure and software needed to process and analyse monumental civic datasets.[17]

By making data public, cities invite more transparency and scrutiny by public agents, which can then broaden the conventional applications of a particular set of data and allow for new and original uses.

McKinsey Global Institute estimated in 2011 that the potential savings at a European level from using big data to improve the overall efficiency of government operations, reduce fraud and error, and strengthen tax collection, could then have amounted to €150–€300 billion a year.[18]

Potential cost-savings from economies of scale and 'whole of government' approaches could be considerable in the developing world too. In Nigeria, with a population of about 170 million, there is an enormous overlap on data collection by the various government bodies handling the management and usage of similar information for different purposes. These include the National Bureau of Statistics, the Federal Road Safety Commission for drivers' licenses and vehicle number-plates, the National Identify Management Commission for national identity records, the National Population Commission in charge of federal demographic data, and the Independent National Electoral Commission for voter registration. But, within the country's fractious politics, each represents a powerful body with its own political constituency.

The UK Office of National Statistics uses Google trends analysis to track migration, as the volume of internet searches in foreign languages correlates well with variations in patterns of immigration. It can assist with other social policy: Google search data reveals obesity patterns in the US because a significant correlation exists between search keywords and body mass index levels.[19]

Combining big data and machine learning is proving effective in allowing citizens and government officials to analyse and compare cities and countries around the world. City officials in Chicago teamed up with Allstate Insurance Company and Civic Consulting Alliance to use to analyse and predict the results of health inspections in restaurants. Each year, the city inspects 9,822 food establishments. Unfortunately, its handful of health inspectors are vastly outnumbered by the city's staggering number of restaurants by a ratio of 470 to 1. To help officials better target the workload, the city deployed machine learning on more than 100,000 of the city's health inspections. Within a two-month trial, the city found establishments with critical violations 7 days earlier on average compared with traditional approaches.

The OECD estimates that the market for public sector information in 2010 was $111 bn., with the economic impacts of its application and use were $500bn. In 2008, with another $20bn. If barriers were removed, skills enhanced and data infrastructure improved.[20] In the UK, for instance, use of big data analytics could save £4bn., and across Europe, open government data can promote public sector efficiency, cutting administrative costs by 15 to 20% and private sector growth, with full use of big data potentially worth 0.5% economic growth.[21] But political pressure is needed to overcome organisational resistance to openness, creating also risks of lobbying and regulatory 'capture.' Big problems also will emerge, not least in that big data technologies require stakeholders to collaborate which will increasingly mean sharing big data across borders. The resulting political and legal issues will raise many political challenges, not least if big data is also seen to pose a new geo-political threat to national security.[22]

The key political concern will increasingly be how big data affects, and is affected by power dynamics, citizens' trust in government, and the legitimacy of the state. For example, without high institutional quality, big data augments low social trust arising from ethno-linguistic diversity.[23] The power of elites and powerful corporations will be expanded by big data if that data can be used to promote self-interest, or may be constrained by big data if that data can be used by elites and business to monitor each other, compete openly and force rival groups towards the common good. This will affect what property rights will emerge over personal information, who will benefit most from big data, and whether big data reinforces power differentials between those with the capacity to collect and analyse big data and those who are simply 'data fodder.'   In short, the question of who collects big data for what purpose will increasingly define politics.

A New 'Gilded Age'?

The past suggests how technology and politics interact.   To understand the mutual inter-connection, by which big data is changing the nature of politics while politics is changing big data and its uses, it is helpful to examine the seemingly similar process that happened during the 'Gilded Age' of 'robber baron' industrialists of America at the end of the 19th and start of the 20th century,

At that time, the rise of huge conglomerates controlling powerful new sectors of the economy such as railways or steel, challenged the authority of the state. As wealth became concentrated in the hands of the few who controlled the new industries, the democratic deficit of ensuing political corruption led to demand for tighter regulation. The eventual outcome was to reconfigure the political process in industrialised countries.

Now, once again, in the 21st century the nation state and its institutions are being reshaped by profound changes in many fields, including in the speed of technological development and unprecedented availability of information. Concentrated power over big data are exacerbating growing inequality of income and undermine that trust. As wealth becomes concentrated in the hands of the few who control the data, so political corruption will almost inevitably follow. Demand for tighter regulation and a suitable variant of competition/anti-trust policy seem inevitable.

BOX 3: a Historical Perspective

The private sector in the last few decades has created a whole new economy through ICT and the resultant big data. With it, the major computer, telephone, internet, and web companies/corporations have acquired extraordinary wealth and political influence that raise concerns about monopolistic tactics, not least control over data that threatens democracy and disempower ordinary citizens.

In the last few decades of the 19th century, many of the greatest names in corporate America were widely regarded as using ruthless and immoral business practices to enrich themselves and promote their own political influence, regardless of wider societal interests. Andrew Carnegie, Henry Clay Frick and Charles M. Schwab all of Pittsburgh and New York, cornered the market in steel; James Buchanan Duke monopolised tobacco production from Durham, North Carolina; George Hearst and his son William Randolph Hearst of California, in mining and then newspapers; Andrew W. Mellon of Pittsburgh and J. P. Morgan of New York ruled in finance; John D. Rockefeller of Cleveland controlled the oil industry; and Edward Henry Harriman and Cornelius Vanderbilt of New York dominated the railroads.

By the end of the 19th century democracy seemed at risk: inequality of both income and political influence grew so extreme that finally the US government felt forced to act: the anti-trust legislation of 1890 eventually led in 1911, under the Presidency of Theodore Roosevelt, to the break-up of Standard Oil, controlled by John D. Rockefeller. The wicked capitalists had finally been subdued.

The American self-image as the land of opportunity and democracy, however, soon led to a re-evaluation of that formative era. *John D. Rockefeller: The Heroic Age of American Enterprise* (1940) by Allan Nevins, *Triumph of American Capitalism* (1942) by Louis Hacker, and *Titan: The Life of John D. Rockefeller, Sr.* (1998) by Ron Chernow reinterpreted 'Robber Barons' like Rockefeller as 'industrial statesmen'. While admittedly ruthless in amassing tremendous power and wealth, their image now metamorphosed into successful entrepreneurs and 'captains of industry' who were portrayed as 'civic patron saints.' Their philanthropy, once seen as the cynical purchase of civic respectability and the assuaging of guilty consciences, was recast as supposedly the product of an innate sense of the social responsibility, that outweighed any alleged unscrupulous, if not outrageously corrupt business practices and political influence, most famously exposed by the 1941 film 'Citizen Cane'.[24]

In the 21st century, will the new generation of 'Robber Barons' in the current era of growing inequality,[25] be the owners of big data – the showy or shadowy Carnegies, Fricks, Schwabs, Dukes, Mellons, Morgans, Rockefellers and Vanderbilts of our day - who control the algorithms that allow companies like Apple, Google, Amazon, MySpace, Flickr, Twitter, Skype, Youtube and Facebook in the US, along with Alibaba, JD.Com, Baidu and TenCent from China, and Yandex from Russia - to dominate the new global economy and social networks, just as once their predecessors had controlled the old industrial economy of steel, tobacco, oil and the railroads?

By 2012, ten of the world's top fifty richest billionaires were Americans (with three from just one company), who had made their wealth from computers and internet technology: Bill Gates, $61bn, Steve Ballmer, $15.7bn and Paul Allen, $14.2bn., all of Microsoft; Larry Ellison of Oracle, $36bn, Michael Bloomberg, $22bn; Larry Page and Sergey Brin of Google, $18.7bn each; Jeff Bezos of Amazon, $18.4bn; Mark Zuckerberg of Facebook, $17.5bn.; and Michael Dell, of the eponymous computer manufacturer, $15.9bn. By 2015, the new economy was becoming internationalised, with the world's wealthiest people including: from China, Jack Ma with $22.7bn., derived from e-commerce, Ma Huateng with $16.1bn from internet media, and Robin Li owning $15.3bn from internet search; while from India, Azim Premji with $19.1bn from software. Oligopoly is on the rise: ten out of the thirteen industrial sectors were more concentrated in 2007 than a decade earlier, and 41% of cash held by big US companies outside the finance sector is owned by tech corporations.

Will big data moguls of the twenty-first century be unscrupulous in exploiting the weak and vulnerable to amass even greater personal fortunes and political muscle? Or will they fear the scorn that once attached to the 'Robber Barons' and aspire to an honourable posterity built from a reputation of admiration and legacy of respect, associated with the Rockefeller Foundation, the Frick Collection, the Carnegie Endowment, or Duke University? Similarly, will "big data philanthropists" emerge to promote "corporate data responsibility" by setting up institutions aimed at sharing big data analytics to protect vulnerable populations and fortify democracy?

Central to effective governance are 'effective institutions' that are impartial (treats all equitably and fairly, essential for building citizens' trust in government), based on ability, and promote continuous learning for incremental change. But effectiveness in an era of big data and growing complexity is not enough. Trustworthiness will increasingly be critical.

At the heart of this complex political relationship is the citizen, voter and taxpayer, employee and consumer, as the informant, the informed and the information of big data. A public is therefore needed that is sufficiently educated about the implications for social cohesion, the stability of democracy and the health of the economy that it can make informed choices to authorise the collection of big data and legitimate its analysis, co-create the policy solutions and be willing to pay taxes to fund the implementation of the findings.

The political leadership will require the capability to frame complex policy choices and make informed decisions in the long-term interest. This is in the wider context of technological innovation as a major driving force in economic growth that requires

Governments to create political support for the process and the opportunities for effectively promoting international competitiveness. But in the wider context of social innovation as a major driving force in political engagement that requires Governments to accept more 'chaotic pluralism' of social media-driven collective action.

The sudden and unprecedented commercial success of Google, Amazon and related internet-based digital, media, and marketing corporations both sprung from and generated big data. This had unexpected but significant consequences. The private sector has been the biggest beneficiary to date of big data and it raises issues about the legitimacy of the potential new forms of immense political influence that companies may be able to exert. Social networking sites encourage popular opinion as individuals exchange and display personal information in a distinct form of Web-based interaction. The politics of the 21st century's 'Gilded Age' of big data will need to define the acceptable degree of political influence exerted by the digital 'robber barons'.

BOX 4: Big Data Ombudspersons by 2020?

A major political debate at the end of the second decade of the 21st century will be around how to protect the common interest in big data, and who will control collection and regulate the ethical code of conduct, including the 'Privacy by Design framework,' in the expertise needed to exploit these data.

Government can only serve as a credible guardian of and catalyst for the legitimacy of big data if it itself is perceived as legitimate. Optimists argue that this strengthens the case for open, transparent and democratic government; pessimists fear an ever-growing digital divide.

Prediction: Offices of Big Data Ombudsmen will be established in 2020 to protect the interests of the citizen whose information has become the engine that fuels the big data revolution. The legislation establishing the post will mandate that its functions include clarifying data ownership and accountability for its use. The core objective of the Ombudsman will be to deepen credibility by building trust and legitimacy. To ensure this, the wealth and political influence derived from freely provided citizen social content will be redistributed to guarantee greater big data equality. A new citizen charter will enable people to obtain answers as to what their data is being used for, who has access to the data and its analysis. The Ombudsman will be required to report to Parliament on legally-binding data protection and privacy policies, protocols for handling citizens' data and terms of usage, the rights of citizens to obtain a copy. They also promote "benefit corporations", a new type of business built on the Internet and, while designed to make money, to be motivated by providing public good.

Inspired by: J. Lanier. 2013. *Who Owns the Future.* New York; World Economic Forum. 2012. *Big Data, Big Impact: New Possibilities for International Development.* Davos.

Chapter 2. Politics of Big Data

Big data offers huge political potential. This potential is evidently both positive and negative. Big data is starting to shape not just day-to-day public service operations, but also new patterns of citizenship through digital social inclusion or political exclusion. That affects the trust of citizens in officials and, therefore, the perceived legitimacy of government. [26] How such dynamics will actually play out, and whether the 'end of politics' that some predict, depends on if, and how, seven challenges over the 'big data revolution' can be overcome and governance through 'effective institutions' emerges the stronger.[27]

1. Contestation

First, the emergence in developing countries of the digital data society creates a complex and changing political contestation over access to new forms of knowledge production and analysis, and competition between commercial, state and public interests. Even the term 'big data' is contested and is creating a new political struggle.[28]

The political contestation and competition among different actors and stakeholders. Expert power will triumph in big data analytics, but from what field of expertise is currently being fiercely contested as old disciplinary silos are challenged by the revolution in information. The potential political impacts of big data include reshaping definitions of politics itself as well as political subjectivity. [29] China is proposing to use big data analytics to determine citizens' credit standing and to utilise that information to direct economic growth across its provinces.[30]

The vested power of different interpretations and solutions also encourages local, national and international administrations in making "open data" available. Fragmentation and the individualisation of data may undermine collective action and deepen the problem of concentrated benefits versus diffuse costs, with political deliberation replaced by a fragmented aggregation of individual views that deepens political inequality.[31]

It remains unclear how far can and do citizens resist big data collection. Social movements are starting to use big data to foster social change.[32] But little research has yet been done on how data activism may affect the dynamics of national and transnational civil society. Political libertarians, worried about internet privacy, mass surveillance and the 'Big Brother' power of big business derived from big data, created 'AdNauseam,' software. By automatically clicking on advertisements, this technology subverts online advertising, thereby rendering futile user tracking, targeting and surveillance.[33]

2. Power and Patronage

Second, the ability to access, analyse and control the results is a tremendous new source of power - in all its forms. Information has always been power, shaped by bureaucratic turf and the political culture of information, citizenship and identity. What gets measured reflects the power dynamics of data and its interpretation; what does not get measured reflects powerlessness.

Seeing Like a State shows the need in government bureaucracy to conceive the world as 'legible,' so ordered, or order-able. The people collecting a data set, and how they choose to do it, directly determines the data set. How big data is defined also defines the expertise that is required to extract meaning and address partiality, contingency and uncertainty. Government agencies and departments have traditionally seen information as power to be hoarded especially to make staff indispensable in the face of downsizing, cost cutting, and rationalisation. Who then controls this big data, uses it for research and writes up the findings for what purposes? This will become more of an issue globally as Target 17.18 of the Sustainable Development Goals (SDGs) commits the UN member countries to: *increase significantly the availability of high-quality, timely and reliable data disaggregated by income, gender, age, race, ethnicity, migratory status, disability, geographic location and other characteristics relevant in national contexts.* The custodianship of data is political when the repositories of data are characteristically unstable. Hence, data leaks in unexpected ways, through human or technical error, hacking, or whistleblowing. The result is often to cause new political contestation.[34]

For the SDGs, this will be particularly pertinent. Some argue that:

> *the current global development data space remains more characterized by gaps, holes and noise than by anything like an emerging corpus of knowledge that could support dramatically heightened impact, much less long-term goals like self-sufficiency or broad participation spelled out by the UN's Data Revolution Group. Big data from mobile phones and internet searches can play a critical role in measuring human need and programmatic impact, but they must be a complement, not a substitute, for program- and policy-relevant data collected purposefully at the appropriate spatial and temporal scale for analysis.[35]*

Data collection is still largely designed in the Global North. Rather than asking decision makers in the South what data they actually need to do their job, then helping them devise efficient ways to collect it, donor agencies are primarily concerned for data that meet their own needs. Progress toward demand-driven, locally-relevant big data in developing countries remains subject to the political requirements of institutions in the developed world: *It would be horribly ironic if the move to Big/Open Data saw citizens become mere data generators – the object of data, rather than the subject.*[36] Applied to development, big data can foster the transformative actions needed to respond to the 2030 agenda, according to how the data are produced and used.

3. Discrimination and Bias

Third, big data, by generating new concentrations of power, creates problems of representativeness precisely because it can be used to discriminate against individuals and groups. Big data cannot account for existing discrimination nor for those who participate in the social world in ways that do not register as digital signals.[37] The more data is expected to answer big questions, the greater the inclination to shape the world into an input that fits into an algorithm.

Big data can exacerbate discrimination, but can also help minorities through data disaggregation that traditional forms cannot offer. By closing data gaps to prevent discrimination and to promote 'transparency' and 'accountability', it can change the way government operate, relationships between people and government officials, and the potential of the 'non-powerful' to participate in the political process.

New media connectivity, including big data, increase the dangers of erroneous political messages, local and national, by playing on stereotypes and superficiality. Furthermore, global data shows that more than 1.7 billion women in low- and middle-income countries do not own mobile phones. The 'digital divide' means poor people use the internet less and rarely to maximum benefit.[38] Similarly, the World Wide Web Foundation study of urban poverty across Africa, Asia and Latin America, concluded that women are nearly 50 per cent less likely to access the internet than men. Yet other research shows that women with an equal level of income, employment and education to men actually use ICT more than their male counterparts. [39] The politics of big data is influenced by the 'digital divide' – who counts depends on who and what is counted.

Big data contribute to the advancement of science, innovation, and learning. To raise concerns about it is to hinder progress if big data can help everyone in the aggregate, even though the data can reveal much that was not intended. [40] Methodologies like sentiment analysis or network analysis of the dynamics of social media are open to misuse. Theories of change locate a programme, project or campaign within a wider analysis of how change comes about. They articulate and challenge our assumptions and acknowledge the influence of wider systems and actors. But crowd-sourcing for example, in the context of the contemporary malaise of politics, inclusiveness and transparency, but fantasises the actual size, composition, internal structures and motivations of the supposed "crowds," with significant implications of citizen initiative processes to the state–citizen relationship.[41]

Increasingly, research is challenging the notion that crowd-sourcing is simply sets of independent individuals who are neatly representative of a larger population. Instead of naivety, research highlights the importance of detailed political economy analysis of the clusters, networks, and power structures inherent within crowdsourcing. This has implications for the democratic legitimacy of all the more naive crowdsourcing processes.[42] In Finland, for example, one citizen initiative ironically ended up decreasing government legitimacy, after the government failed to implement the findings. In more authoritarian contexts, crowdsourcing platforms can be subtly exploited to align 'civil society' with state objectives and prevent independent collective action.[43] The predictive analysis potential of big data already enables accurate targeting of voters, efficient fund-raising, and refining of political messaging. Data scientists could make voting in elections more marginal as a source of feedback, increasing the use of elections as opportunities for citizens to express dissatisfaction rather than shape policy.

This kind of manipulation of and through big data is a political temptation. The simplest of analyses have control of the narrative, rendering critical thinking secondary to the endeavour. The divide between those with access to big data and regular citizens seems to be increasing, at the same time constraining the potential benefits and increasing risk. Dangerous activity is not only possible but inevitable. The efficiency in monitoring data as well as "nudging technologies" points to a form of social engineering, one that tends toward complete acquiescence if unchecked.[44]

How then is trust between citizens and state built? Development requires public service excellence - impartial and meritocratic, able to strengthen citizens' trust and state empowerment by implementing incremental reform through continuous learning (not the 'Tyranny of Normative Expertise'). The potential for infringement of data protection and privacy become increasingly sensitive politically, although citizen-generated data, like big data including social media data, can raise the political influence of citizens by helping to validate governments' own data and offer credible and complementary data in areas where data collection has been weak, but can also be unrepresentative and lack rigor.[45]

No data are free of bias. The collection of data is a subjective process. The presentation of data can be manipulated to answer a specific question or enact a particular political vision. Data is never removed from human bias. Moreover, technology and methodology do not trump human power dynamics. Big data is not in itself an enlightened vehicle for political liberation.

In 2008, the technology magazine *Wired* claimed that: *'[this] is a world where massive amounts of data and applied mathematics replace every other tool that might be brought to bear. Out with every theory of human behaviour, from linguistics to sociology. Forget taxonomy, ontology and psychology. Who knows why people do what they do? The point is they do it, and we can track it and measure it with unprecedented fidelity. With enough data, the numbers speak for themselves.'* [46]

Now it is increasingly clear that numbers do not speak for themselves. The Web is awash with bad big data analytics, spurious correlation and poor analytical practice. By 2013 *Wired* magazine was concluding that *'... Big Data does not automatically yield good analytics'* and insisting that *'Big Data is a tool, but should not be considered the solution'*.

Identifying gaps in research and data collection, as a way of limiting error, is also not an easy task. The 2016 Federal Trade Commission Reports notes that the potential for contributing errors occur at multiple stages, and simply adding more data does not necessarily mean that data is recalibrated closer to an objective truth. More importantly, data complexity muddles the ability to understand underlying features that have specific outcomes. These unknowns affect data in such a way that the final results are not sufficiently representative for policymaking, though still under the guise of an actual depiction of reality. Big data, therefore, can be more subjectively expressive rather than illustrative of society or groups.

The question, then, is rather to understand the impact of the biases on the big data results. 'Pure science' suddenly becomes a covert game of hiding political aims and framing the process. Otherwise, critics warn, the *politics of 'Big Data' can help bring about a self-referential performativity in which the educated upper and middle classes are given a new mirror in which to look at themselves.*[47]

Big data is as affected by hidden intentions, systematic and random errors, partial information or biased visions making this new knowledge as situated and partial as any other type of knowledge. The poor and vulnerable are most affected.[48]

Big data can also suggest policies that are contentious, like crime profiling, requiring political leadership, and algorithm-informed policy suggestions perpetuate the bias within the datasets on which they are based.[49]

4. Technocratic Solutions

Will big data create the perfect toolkit and best-practice guidance to solving many policy challenges, and offer clarity on where to begin, what questions to ask, what success looks like, rather than 'best fit' plans and actions tailored to local context? The mythology of big data is that more data means ever greater accuracy and 'the truth,' that statistical algorithms can find patterns where mere science cannot, so turning numbers into knowledge and thereby putting an end to theory.[50] The data, according to this proposition, determines its own meaning. So big data might seem to be the technocrat's dream and the statistician's nirvana: *"A true data revolution would draw on existing and new sources of data to fully integrate statistics into decision making, promote open access to, and use of, data and ensure increased support for statistical systems."* [51] Through this 'Data Revolution', knowledge is being generated that would seem to be more irrefutable, neutral and objective. As a result, policy-making is becoming rational, incontestable and apolitical. Public service no longer speculates nor hypothesises, nor is it enslaved by ideology. Without the troublesome need for questionable theory or testable hypothesis, policy-based evidence is finally being replaced by evidence-based policy. Accuracy is triumphing as human biases are removed and big data provides policy-makers with the clear scientific patterns exposing the shifting fault-lines in society, the true trends in social, economic, political, and environmental inter-relationships, and the real meaning of change.

Hence, thanks to big data, the 'truth' becomes manifest, albeit revealed less by major flashes of sudden revelation than through the persistent accumulation of insight built on small effects with large aggregate consequences. The availability of both the data and the techniques to mine them make it feasible to individualise policy responses, like Amazon marketing, far beyond the granularity of location, inequalities or ethnicities. Big data's "veracity via volume, variety, and velocity" prevents the possibility of error and offers public service a seductive objectivity and post-modernist certainty for tackling the complex world of social phenomena.

These claims made for big data echo long-standing utopian hopes and political fantasies. Big data, some optimists and idealists declare, will finally deliver Plato's ideal of social harmony abolishing the need for politics, and on the Enlightenment vision of the perfectibility of humanity through rational scientific progress eliminating political contestation.[52] It also eliminates social interaction in the workplace: office politics is killed off by perfect information rendering 'gate-keepers' irrelevant.

5. Complexity and the 'Datafication of Reality'

Fifth, aggregated individual actions cannot illustrate the complicated dynamics of social interaction by which society as a whole is greater than the sum of its parts. Data-driven systems have long been part of business intelligence and performance management, so what is different about bringing these practices to public administration? The Digital Methods Initiative to map the politics of open data as an issue on digital media, surveillance or discrimination, is helping to highlight some of the issues around the politics of user data access, ownership, and control.[53] The lack of theory of digital political economy is preventing efforts to reshape how databases rely on negotiated, abbreviated and contested social concepts, and risks making big data the dominant source on 'reality'. While the mechanisms for collecting, storing and even analysing data have become infinitely more sophisticated, the philosophical, political and economic debates reveal the disjuncture between technology, language and the labelling that shapes the collection and use of data. As the 2014 report to the US President on big data put it: *While big data unquestionably increases the potential of government power to accrue unchecked, it also holds within it solutions that can enhance accountability, privacy, and the rights of citizens.*[54]

"Planning is everything; the plan is nothing," General Eisenhower once observed. As big data exacerbate the asymmetry of power between the state and the people, and perhaps between the private and the public sectors as well as with civil society, a new 'resource curse' around the new asset of information will deepen authoritarianism, or increases the risk of it in countries with weak institutions protecting the rights of citizens. Big data may also encourage the type of arrogant certainty that results in the perverse effects of top-down development programmes and *grandes projets* nicely described in James C. Scott's classic *'Seeing Like a State'* or James Ferguson's *'Anti-Politics Machine'*.

It is, for example, unlikely that Bhutan would abandon its Gross National Happiness (GNH) used by the government's Gross National Happiness Commission to assess or review all draft policies, programmes and projects through a GNH lens, even if it is not the determining factor for ultimately approving or endorsing a policy.

6. Vested Interests

New vested interests will develop around the political groups that big data will make possible. "Thin" citizenship created by technologies that favour the voices of the opinionated will reduce practical experience of the "general will"—that is, a way of figuring out together solutions to complex problems of interdependence. The net result of big data will be to offer personalised and "simplified civic participations options . . . not requir[ing] extensive contemplation of civic affairs" to the less engaged. Personalisation is undermining not just interest in civic life, but even our basic orientation to one another as members of a shared democracy.[55]

The political importance of inclusion and exclusion in big data will grow, along with the risk of political interference. Inclusion will mean being counted, and so securing recognition accompanied by access to resources, but at the risk of becoming a digital abstraction in increasingly complex information systems in which the human seems barely present in the external world. Being excluded from big data, on the other hand, will mean being a new marginalisation. Denied official recognition and rejected for access to resources, marginalised groups have a long history of being deliberately excluded from data yet still being subject to various forms of threat, intimidation and persecution as a threat to the system that is collecting the data. As the UN Secretary-General's Independent Expert Advisory Group report on the data revolution points out:

Fundamental elements of human rights have to be safeguarded: privacy, respect for minorities or data sovereignty requires us to balance the rights of individuals with the benefits of the collective. Much of the new data is collected passively, from the 'digital footprints' people leave behind, from sensor-enabled objects or is inferred via algorithms. The growing gap between the data people actively offer and the amounts of "massive and passive" data being generated and mediated by third parties fuels anxiety ...that the data could be used to harm, rather than to help. People could be harmed in material ways, if the huge amount that can be known about people's movements, their likes and dislikes, their social interactions and relationships is used with malicious intent ...[56]

Companies collect, process, analyse and use big data to achieve their business objectives in ways that give them greater political clout. Governments may be bound by strict laws about what data it can collect on individuals but big business can privatise the authoritarian surveillance state. As one study warns: *In the absence of a matching skill in government policy, the danger is that those technological changes are leading us down a road to serfdom.*[57]

Vested interest need not always distort the political process. Big data is a potentially powerful tool for transparency. It can uncover previously-unknown correlations, perhaps causality, suggesting fraud and bribery in public procurement. The Open Contracting Data Standard encourages governments to release public procurement data, and open up corporate registries for public analysis. open data initiatives of big data to fight against corruption by institution (eg. the 'Checkbook NYC' portal established by the Comptroller of the City of New York), by sector (such as petroleum and gas, through 'OpenOil') and by theme (such as 'OpenAid,' part of the International Aid Transparency Initiative). The App 'iPaidABribe' allows citizens to report corrupt officials.[58]

7. The politics of the 'apolitical'

Seventh, how big data is generated and shaped, understood, operationalized, and resisted shows contested and multifaceted nature of the 'apolitical politics' of big data. The risks of customization eliminating common political apparatus ties in with the 4th Challenge, of technocratic solutions. The institutional and methodological preconditions of big data as an effective predictor of social behaviour demonstrate how big data practices have the potential to undermine the public sphere. When content—journalistic or otherwise—is tailored to individuals based upon the needs of advertisers and content providers, it fractures the shared political and social life and "risks eliminating the connective media necessary for an effective democracy." The unexpected negative externalities that result from "successful" applications of big data analysis have the potential to undermine fundamental societal structures more than poorly implemented big data initiatives. The seemingly basic question of "in which city were you born?" belies the complexity of the answer "St Petersburg/ Petrograd/ Leningrad/St Petersburg".

Social media can be illusory and biased in revealing overall public sentiment, echoing the 3rd Challenge, of discrimination and bias. Social media, being heavily biased in its coverage of socio-political spaces, turns out often to be a poor predictor of electoral success. Analysis of Twitter profiles and content, such as the Media Standards Trust/King's College London big data analysis of candidates and political influences on Twitter during the UK General Election campaign in 2015 confirmed that such data has genuine potential but also distinct limitations for better understanding of political and social phenomena.[59] Although often claimed as an indicator of a political 'pulse', in fact social media, so far at least, is more reactive in the context of elections rather than predictive. Applying sentiment analysis and other methods to election-related social media data such as Twitter produces results that are surprisingly neutral towards candidates. Yet the aspiration that social media can easily reveal public sentiment towards candidates, and serve as a replacement to polling, remains illusory. In this way, the reputation of big data precedes it, however, has the effect of masking arguably inherent political tendencies.

BOX 5: Big Data in International Development

If big data holds considerable potential at the national level, could big data, or perhaps more accurately 'Big, Open Data' resolve some of the biggest puzzles in the international arena too, perhaps shaping development over the decades to come? In developing countries, the appetite for data in the post-independence era was shaped by the nature of colonial rule, the existence of pre-colonial bureaucracies and the interaction with local, often informal, institutions.

To enable well-informed decision-making and support the implementation of the 2030 Agenda, timely, relevant and high-quality information is needed to foster and monitor development progress. Despite significant efforts so far, critical data are still lacking and knowledge gaps remain, with baseline information concerning many people and groups, particularly the most vulnerable and marginalized, still not being measured. More data needs to be available at the level of disaggregation, including by gender, age, income, location, education or disability, to inform policymakers about allocations or monitoring of outcomes within and between countries, as well as across regions. To be able to monitor and achieve the SDGs, the capacity of governments, private and public institutions and individuals to deliver and use these data will require new and unique political checks and balances, and citizens empowered to use big data to hold governments, companies and international organizations to account.

The emergence in recent years of big data is already making a significant impact.

Mobile phone call data has been used to track population displacement after earthquakes, to model the spread of infectious diseases, and to detect small-scale violence in countries in conflict. Mobile phone connections in Africa are predicted to rise from 564 million in 2013 to 947 million by 2020.

UNDP is working with the Tunisian National Statistics Institute to explore how big and non-traditional sources of data, like social media, can contribute to the establishment of a baseline, and monitoring of progress in achieving the Sustainable Development Goal 16 on peace, justice and good governance.

UNFPA is using big data analysis of social media to understand attitudes towards family planning in Uganda where, with low uptake of contraceptives and a young population (70%), teenage pregnancy (24%) is a significant problem.

UNICEF has used social media monitoring tools to track attitudes towards vaccine hesitancy in Eastern Europe and educate parents to make informed choices. The "Mosquito Abatement Decision Information System" uses satellite data imagery to alert ministries of health to outbreaks of mosquitoes even before they hatch. Satellite remote sensing data is also showing how rainfall affects migration as well as food and livelihood security across Africa.

Internet search data reveals popular sentiment or concern: Colombia's Ministry of Finance uses the information generated by Google searches to assess short-term macroeconomic trends in the country. The Brazilian state of Minas Gerais is using big data to track its progress against that of the whole country.[60] Internet text analysis enables sentiment analysis (e.g. favourable/unfavourable views on a policy) and also lexical analysis: one finding was that the concept of honour in the Middle East changed in response to 9/11.

The use of 'big data' in the Africa Regional Integration Index, jointly developed by the Economic Commission for Africa, the African Union and the African Development Bank to check the performance of countries and their regional economic communities, is summarizing information from more than seventy indicators, to track progress, identify bottlenecks, inform policy decisions and help with future trade negotiations.

During the Haiti earthquake in 2010, emergency services used a bilingual volunteer workforce for translation, tagging, and geocoding information then forwarded to Ushahidi, a website initially developed to map reports of violence in Kenya now turned a global crowdsourcing platform with humanitarian goals, to provide accurate coordinates to the search and rescue teams on the ground.

All these efforts are addressing some of the trickiest political challenges of our time – in an unceasingly unequal world, how to tackle inequality, injustice and bad governance. And, if internet access in developing countries matched that of the developed world, $2.2 trillion in GDP and 140 million jobs would be created.[61]

On the potential impacts on international development, see: World Economic Forum. 2012. *Big Data, Big Impact: New Possibilities for International Development*; and United Nations Global Pulse.2013. *Big Data for Development: A primer.*

Chapter 3. Institutions and Big Data

Effective institutions for Big Data Politics

These seven factors will influence the use of data at every level of government but will be more pronounced in national politics where public servants lack the skills to interpret data properly and still instinctively are more concerned for national security than openness. *They should stop being gatekeepers, guarding government data, and become enablers encouraging its wider use; key to this will be the development of a wider understanding of data issues.*[62]

Effective institutions are the key determinant of development;[63] and essential for a functioning and stable democracy. [64] The effective administrative capability of the state is an important dimension of the 'effective institutions' for public service that shape the most basic functions of the state. The evidence for its importance includes a close statistical connection between the quality of public bureaucracy and economic growth, with merit-based recruitment, promotion from within and career stability being key determinants.[65] While a skilled, motivated and efficient public service with a professional ethos will be only a necessary but not sufficient, condition for good governance, an ineffective or inefficient public service is certainly sufficient to produce bad governance.[66]

The public service will need to be able to manage the transition over the coming decade, tied to regulating the private and public sector 'big data' usage for the common good, through impartial, meritocratic and 'common sense' behaviours that inspire citizens' trust. The public, however, must also be concerned that big data manipulation by the private sector creating a yet unacknowledged crisis if an underpaid and under-resourced public service in both developing and developed countries, cannot match the capacity of private corporations. The potential impact this would have on subverting public welfare and adding to the demoralisation and demotivation of the public sector, will prove politically significant.

Currently, therefore, cities are perhaps the more prominent users of big data, boosting the 'If Mayors Ruled the World' image of local urban government as being on a scale that allows it to be more competent and responsive than its national equivalent – and perhaps part of the success of small states. The rise of global smart cities includes the efforts of the city-states of Singapore and Abu Dhabi to become international data analytics hubs. [67] Cross-border aspects of big data will include to what extent should governments be open in sharing data at the internationally, and how can inequalities between states not be exacerbated by exclusivity of access to big data or capacity to analyse it.

In communities, big data will appear more problem-solving (e.g.. most efficient route to collect the garbage) and less threatening to misuse and potential abuse of human rights, data protection and personal privacy. IBM has been working in Rio de Janeiro, Dublin, New

York, Zhenjiang, Chicago and Stockholm to improve emergency services response, the movement of traffic and public transportation systems, and the supply of power and water. The Office of Policy and Strategic Planning in the Office of the Mayor of New York City is applying predictive data analytics to discover tax evasion on cigarette sales and illegal waste disposal, and is sharing this expertise with Boston, Chicago and Philadelphia.

Internationally, big data resembles the nuclear industry in the 1950s – the huge potential was appreciated but deep concerns over potential risks were recognised, so UN set up the IAEA in 1957 in response to these fears and expectations generated by nuclear technology following U.S. President Eisenhower's "Atoms for Peace" address to the General Assembly of the United Nations on 8 December 1953.

The public service has traditionally used its authority to extract data as required on local social, environmental and economic trends to inform central decision-making. If the people who are the subjects of the data are politically weak, the more they might benefit from the insights, if presented right. But political powerlessness means that they are rarely involved further in interpretation or use. The politics of access reflects the public service relation with citizenry as the product of underlying social forces and history, so 'Public Management' type reforms that focus on technical or managerial issues while ignoring politics and historical heritage, invariably fail. Effective institutions, good government and good governance are premised on and, in many ways synonymous with, an efficient and effective public service. [68] It establishes the enabling environment for social, political and economic development, by giving governments the capability to plan for the long-term, and formulate and implement policies, strategies and programmes that deliver public goods and services, policy improvements, sustainable management of public expenditure and revenue, sustainable management of the environment, as well as institutional development to entrench better ways of working.[69]

BOX 6: the Politics of the First 'Big Data' Revolution

This is not the first 'big data' revolution but the second.

The first occurred in the 19th century with the explosion in data collection – the 'avalanche of numbers'. In the United Kingdom, for instance, government began collecting data on an unprecedented scale, and publishing it in parliamentary Blue Books. The risk of overload due to the lack of analytical capacity stimulated new techniques for presenting these large and complex quantities of data through data visualisation and social mapping innovations, such as William Playfair's line graph, bar and pie charts, and Florence Nightingale's polar diagrams. Charles Babbage (1791-1871) attempted to build the world's first computer to help analyse the data collected.

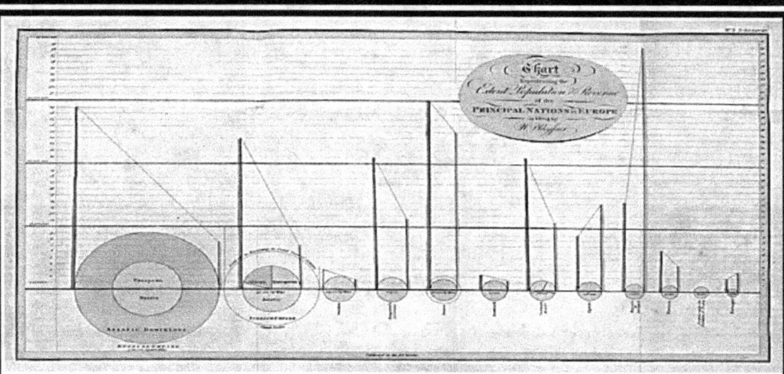

The 19th century data visualization revolution.

The result of the first big data era was the 'probabilisation' of western politics and policy making. Statistical explanation imposed order on chaos, but at the cost of strengthening political control and state intervention, and lessening expectations of individual freedom.

Inspired by I. Hacking. 1975. *The Emergence of Probability*. Cambridge; and I. Hacking. 1990. *The Taming of Chance*. Cambridge.

However, new forms of data will revise or deepen that dimension to the citizen-state-public service interface. If politicians and bureaucrats are incentivised to use big data in different ways (that is, to make political arguments, or to assess potential policies), they can prevent each other from engaging in corruption and instead stimulate good and effective governance.

But big data can also amplify the repercussions and implications of poor data quality if recorded data is erroneous, miscoded, fragmented, or incomplete. Big data will affect not just the quality of government but also the careers of politicians and bureaucrats. A high level of meritocracy co-varies strongly with low corruption, how efficiently state resources are used, and whether the state is capable of reforming public administration to improve it, rather than letting it become a vehicle for capture by vested interests.[70]

Big data alters these dynamics in different ways. While public servants in a neutral bureaucracy seek to keep political conflicts within the policy-making arena, in a politicised bureaucratic apparatus they have an interest in engaging big data for political ends to enhance their career prospects. The result could be an escalation and proliferation of political conflict within state agencies and with the public interacting with them.[71]

Big data also reshapes how *Wu-wei,* or the ancient bureaucratic art of purposeful inaction, an ancient Taoist concept signifying more than studied fatalism, can express the professional harmony in which a bureaucrat's decisions and actions, while recognising the limitations of public authority, flow in spontaneous accord with the context.[72] Above all, the abiding skill of public service – applied common sense – will be fortified or fragmented by big data. The political economy of development goals in any context will shape the potential use and impact of big data.

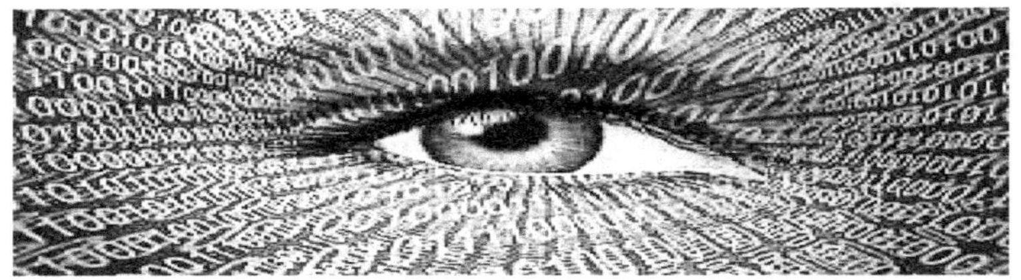

The Politics of Paranoia: Big Data for Big Brother?

The result is deepening democratic governance revolutionized by the big data now being generated every day. 'Algorithmic regulation' or enforcement of rules and laws by monitoring behaviours such as through mobile phones is increasingly feasible. <u>Not</u> possessing a mobile phone will then become deeply suspicious. Surveillance using big data methodologies can be useful: for instance, the riskiest group of drivers, young males, will reduce their dangerous driving behaviour by up to 72 percent if they know that they are being monitored. After the Boston Marathon bombing in 2013, big data technologies enabled the swift arrest of the guilty through the rapid analysis of more than 480,000 images to identify suspicious patterns of behaviour.[73]

But equally, unprecedented state and private surveillance capacities are potentially open to misuse. An article written by a member of the propaganda department committee at University of Electronic Science and Technology in Chengdu and published in October 2015 in *Studies in Ideological Education*, a journal issued by China's education ministry, suggested using big data to track the political views of individual university students by creating a "political ideology database" from library records, surveys, social media, and other sources to collect "quantifiable, accurate, and personalized information" and "improve the effectiveness of ideological education." In 2015 details of the British security service's "Karma Police" programme became public, showing comprehensive screening of Internet use.[74]

The Snowden/NSA and 'Wiki-leaks' affairs had already intensified fears of 'Big Data for Big Brother', that totalitarian surveillance techniques of the isolated individual living in the Kafka-esque state were becoming ever more invasive.[75] The 2015 report on big data for the European Parliament calls for strengthening the rights of digital citizens, given *the high degree of opacity of many contemporary data processing activities directly affects the right of the individuals to know what is being done with the data collected about them.* [76] As the 2014 report to the US President on big data put it: *Properly implemented, big data will become an historic driver of progress, helping our nation perpetuate the civic and economic dynamism that has long been its hallmark. Big data technologies will be transformative in every sphere of life. The knowledge discovery they make possible raises considerable questions about how our framework for privacy protection applies ... big data analytics have the potential to eclipse longstanding civil rights protections in how personal information is used in housing, credit, employment, health, education, and the marketplace.* [77]

But 'big data' paranoia is a conjoined twin: the anxiety of the citizen under surveillance is matched by the anxiety of the surveillance state: the more the authorities know the known knowns, the more they worry about the unknown unknowns. As the old joke says: the fact that you are not paranoid doesn't mean that they are not out to get you! [78]

Chapter 4: Big Data Politics in the Future

A new politics is emerging. Big data will alter incentives, opportunities and risks. The potential of big data to enable the customisation of interactions and services in both the public and private sector carries the spolitical risks of reinforcing biases, stereotypes, and value judgements. To prevent this, politicians must articulate a new social contract developed by public sector regulators, private sector operators and civil society.

One result may be a greater focus on the political salience of cities. Singapore and South Korea are promoting 'Smart City'/'Smart Nation' big data uses abroad, such as in the Ukraine where Seoul helped Kiev improve their bus systems with big data.

Politics and public service at national or sub-national level are the product of context, but could the rise of 'big data' mark the 'End of Politics'? Such an outcome might seem possible if big data creates only one possible choice of rational action, that triumph for evidence-based policy would spell the death knell for political debate. This would mean ignoring the historians, politicians and political scientists, as well as all the 'old data' experience. The current euphoria for the potential of big data will mature into a balanced understanding of its strengths and limitations. It will take time. As Charles Mackay in his classic work *Extraordinary Popular Delusions and the Madness of Crowds*, first pointed out in 1841: "Men, it has been well said, think in herds; it will be seen that they go mad in herds, while they only recover their senses slowly, and one by one."[79] It will be the effectiveness of public institutions, not the computational potential of big data that will shape how politics evolves – but it will survive big data. Human biases will continue to structure scientific understanding of patterns in trends and meaning of social, political and economic and historical contexts. Big data will create spurious correlations, reflecting the values and objectives of data producers and analysts.[80]

For public service, the challenge will be whether the organisational politics will really allow or encourage free-thinkers to ponder the unknown unknowns created by complexities that interact in ways that defy a deterministic, linear analysis. When General Matthew B.

Ridgway, the U.S. Army Chief of Staff in the mid-1950s, was asked what he thought was his most important role as the nation's top soldier, he answered, "To protect the mavericks." What Ridgway meant was that a future war might be completely different from that currently envisaged on which plans were being made. The mavericks were an essential asset for challenging dominant 'group-think' orthodoxy and, by seeing the future differently and hopefully more correctly, would reduce the risk of another 'Pearl Harbor'.[81]

Big data can likewise generate new knowledge for policy-making but big data's collection, analysis and use will still be framed by political choice. So long as people are not 'rational' and do not behave 'predictably,' then the hope of apolitical data usage will remain merely the technocrat's dream. Public service will continue to reflect the ideologies and personalities of its political leadership. Where human systems are complex, contradictory and paradoxical, then data generated knowledge will remain refutable and contestable. The perfect knowledge assumed by big data is one of its big flaws, by seeing the solution to every problem as more data.

The political and practical challenge will increasingly be how to bring together private sector methodologies, public administrative expertise and the political leadership needed to apply big datasets to public sector decision-making in an effective, efficient but also equitable manner. The politics of big data will be shaped by power struggles over how big data influences perceived 'fairness' in resource mobilisation and allocation. Mass political movements will tend to fragment in the face of more differentiated policy responses.

Personalized information builds a "filter bubble" or digital prison limiting the capacity of citizens to formulate political opinion. So political debate will focus on the validity of evidence and the methodologies used in data analysis, and on how to contextualise new findings in relation to other information, conflicting theories and contested policies, where small data studies and historical experience are also needed to make sense of the new emerging patterns. Appointed officials and elected politicians will need to cooperate in applying big data in improving public organizations. How these dynamics will strengthen or undermine the influence of either, and the trust of citizens in government and therefore its perceived legitimacy, is unclear. The challenge then, will be how to manage.

BOX 7: the 'Dictatorship of Big Data': Big Meaningless Metrics, Big Political Risk?

The public policy risks arising from over-reliance on numbers is exemplified by how the use, abuse, and misuse of data by the U.S. military during the Vietnam War culminated in the defeat of the world's superpower by an extremely poor, badly equipped but highly motivated enemy.

Robert McNamara, the U.S. secretary of defense from 1961 to 1968, believed that data, subjected to statistical rigor and logical analysis, would ensure that decision makers could understand a complex situation, plan rationally and make the right choices – as had worked well when he was President of Ford Motor Corporation. The world, correctly tidied up through delineated, denoted, demarcated, and quantified data, would reveal the 'Truth,' regardless of the complex, ill-defined and interdependent nature of 'irrational', messy political problems.

McNamara argued that the key statistic in the Vietnam War was the "body count": kill enough Viet Cong and Ho Chi Minh would give up. But the data on enemy deaths ignored enemy motivation and morale: fighting an 'army of occupation', the Vietnamese had an almost limitless supply of 'bodies'.

> So data, big or not, will always be deceptive if of poor quality, biased, misanalysed, misleading, or misunderstood, and especially risky when the data is not capturing what it purports to quantify.[82]

The formulation and upholding of big data policy will depend on an impartial, ethical and capable public service. But the biggest political threat to the use of big data may be the culture of 'evidence-based policy' – that evidence is simply ignored if it does not fit an existing world view. A lack of concern for facts is evident in political campaigns and sound bites. Because data has never been so good, the answer to many problems has never been so complex, especially for social problems without simplistic answers. Yet politicians demand the 'killer statistic,' the media seek a pithy fact, the public cherish the moral certainty of a simple number. Indifference to big data and its potential would be a tragedy.

Conclusion

Two and a half thousand years ago, Greek philosopher Heraclitus noted, "There is nothing permanent except change." Big data will prove to be a fundamental transformation in information technology and the political dynamics around this should be understood but, in its politics, not just its impact on politics, how profoundly will that technological change prove to be?

The lesson from progress since the sixth century BC suggests that things technological are also often political. The change wrought by big data will, like any disruptive technology, affect power relations and so prove to be highly political, with profound impacts on government, public administration, politics and governance generally. Big data works in the public interest best when effective institutions bring together private sector experts, public officials, activists and data scientists to combine skills, expertise, foresight and insights to catalyse reform.

The potential of big data is clear. The increasing capacity, in an ever-growing number of fields, to use big data to detect and act on variation where fine-grained differentiation – between people, things, ideas or situations – has historically been difficult and costly, will change power dynamics. Governments, like the private sector, are indeed being transformed through the implementation of new online platforms, web analytic and user research techniques, 'agile' management methods, and the introduction of design principles.

But potential risks are also evident. The big data and ICT revolutions will mean that scientific 'facts', human values, and politics principles become more blurred. A political theory of big data is needed to understand the subjectivity of data and promote information justice, both distributive and relational, to bring about social change. The concept of government and politics could be reimagined, with citizens 'reconfigured' as users of 'government' understood as a standardized platform for services, subject to continuous performance measures and data analysis, while offering unparalleled opportunities for new forms of political engagement.[83]

The political importance attached to education will grow, to ensure adaptability to a rapidly changing environment to safeguard livelihoods, contain human biases, misuses and abuses, and guarantee political rights. Citizens will require the capacity to ask the right questions and evaluate the credibility of political policies.

Governments will only be able to uphold the credibility of big data if they themselves are perceived as legitimate. Effective use of big data depends on effective institutions – which are deeply rooted in history and core principles of impartiality, meritocracy and trust needed to address the deeply-rooted human desire for certainty to allay primordial fears about the future:

> *... as we know, there are known knowns; there are things we know we know. We also know there are known unknowns; that is to say we know there are some things we do not know. But there are also unknown unknowns – the ones we don't know we don't know. And if one looks throughout the history of our country and other free countries, it is the latter category that tend to be the difficult ones.*[84]

The debate over the politics of big data is just beginning, but it will mirror the ambition for good governance: in the words of American

political commentator and Nobel Prize winner
Bob Dylan, presciently penned fifty years ago:

As the present now will later be past
The order is rapidly fadin'
And the first one now will later be last
For the times they are a-changin'.

Endnotes

[1] AI is already being shown to exacerbate discrimination: eg.:
https://points.datasociety.net/uncertainty-edd5caf8981b;
https://www.theguardian.com/technology/2016/dec/19/discriminat
ion-by-algorithm-scientists-devise-test-to-detect-ai-
bias?utm_source=esp&utm_medium=Email&utm_campaign=GU+Tod
ay+main+NEW+H+categories&utm_term=204928&subid=5675695&C
MP=EMCNEWEML661912; and
http://approximatelycorrect.com/2016/11/07/the-foundations-of-
algorithmic-bias/

[2] The concept of "Big Data" was first proposed by M. Cox and D.
Ellsworth. 1997. Managing big data for scientific visualization. *ACM
Siggraph*, p.235; for general background, see V. Mayer-Schönberger
and K. Cukier. 2013. *Big Data: A Revolution that Will Transform how
We Live, Work, and Think*. Houghton Mifflin Harcourt.

[3] Remote data collection companies are pioneering methods to "crowd-
seed" local data collection from mobile phones for a range of interests.

[4] Mosco, V. (2014) *To the Cloud: Big Data in a Turbulent World*. New
York.

[5] The data revolution is used as a term to describe the surge in the
volume of data, described above. It has also been used to describe the
need for better data, eg. http://www.undatarevolution.org/data-
revolution/

[6] United Nations. 2014. *A World That Counts: Mobilising The Data
Revolution for Sustainable Development*; the White House. 2014. *Big
Data: Seizing Opportunities, Preserving Values*; the White House.
2015. *Big Data and Differential Pricing;* the European Parliament.
2015. *Big Data and Smart Devices and Their Impact on Policy.*

[7] http://smartcitiescouncil.com/article/battling-traffic-jams-smarter-
traffic-signals, accessed 23 December 2015.

[8] M. Meeker and Liang Yu. 2013. *Internet Trends,* Kleiner Perkins
Caulfield Byers.

[9] A. Hassanien, A. Azar, V. Snasel, J. Kacprzyk, and J. Abawajy.
2015. *Big Data in Complex Systems: Challenges and Opportunities*. p.
420.

[10] A. Aggarwal. 2016. Opportunities and Challenges of Big Data in
Public Sector, in: A. Aggarwal (ed.) *Managing Big Data Integration in
the Public Sector*. Harrisburg.

[11] H. Ekbia, Mattioli, M., Kouper, I., Arave, G., Ghazinejad, A.,
Bowman, T., Suri, V., Tsou, A., Weingart, S. and C. Sugimoto. 2015.
Big data, bigger dilemmas: A critical review. *Journal of the Association
for Information Science and Technology*, 66: 1523–1545. It is also
changing political behaviours: eg. But evaluating loyalty and
disloyalty used to be an entirely subjective exercise … The era of Big

Data is changing all that. .... When you've crossed and been crossed by so many people in 35 years of bare-knuckle politics, it's naturally hard to keep track of all the slights. What better than a computer scorecard that replaces the old mental tally of friends and enemies? http://bigdata-madesimple.com/big-data-makes-for-meaner-politics/#sthash.OYt2w565.dpuf

[12] Weiss, C. H. (1979). The many meanings of research utilization, *Public Administration*, 39(5): 426–431.

[13] Eg. over methodologies to measure public sector output and productivity: eg. UK Parliament. 2014.
Public Administration Committee. *Fourth Special Report. Caught red-handed: Why we can't count on Police Recorded Crime statistics.* London.

[14] Tufekci, Z. (2014). Engineering the Public: Big Data, Surveillance and Computational Politics. *First Monday.*
http://firstmonday.org/ojs/index.php/fm/article/view/4901/4097.

[15]

https://advertising.microsoft.com/en/WWDocs/User/display/cl/researchreport/31966/en/microsoft-attention-spans-research-report.pdf

[16] H. Margetts et al. 2016. Political Turbulence: How Social Media Shape Collective Action. Princeton, pp.226-7.

[17] http://www.informationweek.com/government/big-data-analytics/big-data-poses-challenges-for-federal-agencies/d/d-id/1322525

[18] Report: *Big Data: The Next Frontier for Innovation, Competition and Productivity.*

[19] S. Sarigul. 2014. *Nowcasting Obesity in the U.S. Using Google Search Volume Data.* Paper presented to the Agricultural and Applied Economics Association Symposium: Social Networks, Social Media and the Economics of Food, May 2014, Montreal.

[20] OECD. 2015. Data-Driven Innovation. Paris, p.404.

[21] OECD 2015 op. cit., p.409.

[22] http://thehill.com/blogs/congress-blog/technology/257655-big-data-bad-actors

[23] N. Charron & B. Rothstein 2014. Social Trust, Quality of Government and Ethnic Diversity. *Working Paper 2014:20,* The Quality of Government Institute, University of Gothenburg.

[24] Based on the life of Randolph Heart. To try to prevent the film's release, Hearst's representatives began gathering information on the private life of the film's director, Orson Welles, while Senator Burton K. Wheeler hinted that a Congressional investigation of "un-American" influences in Hollywood would result. A member of the Rockefeller family acting for Hearst then convinced Louis B. Mayer of Metro-Goldwyn-Mayer (MGM) Studios to offer to buy the film from its producers, R.K.O. Pictures, so that it could be destroyed and not released. Welles, however, had White House support because of the film's overt backing for President Franklin D. Roosevelt's effort to win over public opinion to end isolationism and enter World War II, and

had already privately screened it for enough influential people by that time that R.K.O. felt forced to release it: see R. Carringer. 1985. *The Making of Citizen Kane*. Berkeley and Los Angeles: University of California Press.

[25] See T. Picketty. 2014. *Capital in the 21st Century*. London, passim.

[26] Eg. https://www.theguardian.com/technology/2017/may/07/the-great-british-brexit-robbery-hijacked-democracy suggests that big data was used to influence the UK's Brexit referendum in 2016.

[27] See the work of the Effective Institutions Platform, jointly run by the OECD-DAC and the GCPSE.

[28] Crawford, K. 2013. The hidden biases in big data. *Harvard Business Review*: see http://blogs.hbr.org/2013/04/the-hidden-biases-in-big-data

[29] S. Ansolabehere and E. Hersh. 2012. Validation: What Big Data Reveal about Survey Misreporting and the Real Electorate. *Political Analysis* 20(4): 437-459.

[30] https://www.economist.com/news/briefing/21711902-worrying-implications-its-social-credit-project-china-invents-digital-totalitarian

[31] The problem famously elaborated by Mancur Olson in 1965, *The Logic of Collective Action: Public Goods and the Theory of Groups*.

[32] For example, Global Forest Watch, http://www.globalforestwatch.org/

[33] In January 2017 Google, that derives its income from advertising, removed AdNauseam from its Chrome Web Store, and flagged the application as malware.

[34] Lazer, D., R. Kennedy, G. King, and A. Vespignani. 2014. The Parable of Google Flu: Traps in Big Data Analysis. *Science*, 343: 1203-1205.

[35] *http://goal18.org/2015/08/10/data-revolution-we-need/*

[36] *https://oxfamblogs.org/fp2p/the-politics-of-data-the-bit-the-geeks-forget/* October 2015.

[37] Barocas, S. and Selbst, A. 2015. Big Data's Disparate Impact. *California Law Review*, Vol. 104.

[38] The GSMA *Connected Women* report 2015.

[39] *http://www.scidev.net/global/data/editorials/data-gender-ict-digital-divide.html* 2015.

[40] A. Berinsky, G. Huber, and G. Lenz. 2012. Evaluating Online Labor Markets for Experimental Research: Amazon.com's Mechanical Turk. *Political Analysis* 20(3): 351-368.

[41] Heikka, T. 2015. The Rise of the Mediating Citizen: Time, Space and Citizenship in the Crowdsourcing of Finnish Legislation. *Policy & Internet,* 7(3).

[42] Gruzd, A. and K. Tsyganova. 2015. Information Wars and Online Activism during the 2013/2014 Crisis in Ukraine. *Policy & Internet,* 7 (2) 121–158.

[43] Asmolov, G. 2105. Vertical Crowdsourcing in Russia: Balancing Governance of Crowds and State–Citizen Partnership in Emergency Situations. *Policy & Internet,* 7 (3).

[44] https://www.theguardian.com/commentisfree/2017/mar/06/big-data-cambridge-analytica-democracy

[45] *http://civicus.org/images/citizen-generated%20data%20and%20governments.pdf*

[46] On the lack of research on causal connections, see: https://www.ft.com/content/21a6e7d8-b479-11e3-a09a-00144feabdc0 that notes: "a theory-free analysis of mere correlations is inevitably fragile. If you have no idea what is behind a correlation, you have no idea what might cause that correlation to break down."

[47] Burrows, R. and M. Savage. 2014. After the Crisis? Big Data and the methodological challenges of empirical sociology. *Big Data & Society* 1.1, 233-245.

[48] Eg. *http://www.newappsblog.com/2014/12/big-data-and-the-hyper-reserve-army.html#more* 2014.

[49] http://queue.acm.org/detail.cfm?id=2460278

[50] Eg. C. O'Neil. 2016. *Weapons of Math Destruction: How Big Data Increases Inequality and Threatens Democracy.* New York.

[51] *UN High Level Panel Report on International Development.* 2014, p.23

[52] E.g. D. Gauthier. 1990. *Moral Dealing: Contract, Ethics, and Reason.* Cornell University Press.

[53] Puschmann, C. and J. Burgess. 2013. *The Politics of Twitter Data.* HIIG Discussion Paper No. 2013-01.

[54] *Big Data: Seizing Opportunities, Preserving Values.* Washington DC, p.3.

[55] Z. Papacharissi. 2010. *A private sphere: Democracy in a digital age.* Cambridge, UK: Polity, p.107.

[56] *A World That Counts: Mobilising The Data Revolution for Sustainable Development,* p. 7.

[57] D. Colander and R. Kupers. 2014. *Complexity and the Art of Public Policy.* Princeton, p. 149.

[58] Transparency International "Can Big Data Solve the World's Problems, Including Corruption?" and "The Potential of Fighting Corruption through Data Mining." Ernst & Young: "Anti-Corruption Compliance Now Requires Big Data Analytics."

[59] Tufekci, Z. 2014. Big questions for social media big data: Representativeness, validity and other methodological pitfalls. *arXiv preprint arXiv:*1403.7400.

[60] See http://en.dataviva.info/

[61] HDR 2015, p.89.

[62] UK Parliament Public Administration committee. 2014. Report on *Statistics and Open Data: Harvesting unused knowledge, empowering citizens and improving public services.* London, para. 116.

[63] North, 1990; Evans et al. 1999; Rodrik, Subramanian and Trebbi, 2004

[64] Wang, 2003.

[65] Rauch and Evans, 2000

[66] Schiavo-Campo and Sundaram, 2001

[67] Malta and Finland are all good examples of small states making extensive use of big data.

[68] L. Pritchett, M. Woolcock and M. Andrews. 2010. *Capability Traps? The Mechanisms of Persistent Implementation Failure.* CGD Working Paper 234. Washington DC.

[69] A parallel argument is made with regards to Human Resource Management (HRM) and its impact on organisational performance: W. McCourt. 2006.

[70] Dahlström, C, V. Lapuente & J. Teorell. 2012. The Merit of Meritocratization: Politics, Bureaucracy and the Institutional Deterrents of Corruption. *Political Research Quarterly* 65: 658-670.

[71] Dahlström, C. & V. Lapuente. 2010. Explaining Cross-Country Differences in Performance-Related Pay in the Public Sector. *Journal of Public Administration Research and Theory*, 20(3): 577-600.

[72] M. Everest-Phillips. 2015. *International Journal of Civil Service Reform and Practice,*

[73] Mosco, V. (2014) To the Cloud: Big Data in a Turbulent World, New York: Paradigm.

[74] D. Helbing, B. Frey, G. Gigerenzer, E. Hafen, M. Hagner, Y. Hofstetter, J. van den Hoven, R. Zicari, A. Zwitter. *Will Democracy Survive Big Data and Artificial Intelligence?* Scientific American, February 25, 2017; *Big data, meet Big Brother: China invents the digital totalitarian state. The worrying implications of its social-credit project.* The Economist (December 17, 2016).

[75] Edward Snowden, a contractor for the US National Security Agency, in 2013 revealed a US government global big data signals surveillance programme; In George Orwell's novel Nineteen Eighty-Four, Big Brother is the leader of a totalitarian state where the slogan "Big Brother is watching you" expresses government by mass surveillance.

[76] *Op.cit*, p.4.

[77] Op. cit., p.3.

[78] K. Crawford. 2014. The Anxieties of Big Data. *The New Inquiry* (30 May).

[79] *Op. cit.*, p.143.

[80] R. Kitchin. 2014. Big Data, new epistemologies and paradigm shifts. *Big Data & Society* 1.1.

[81] Quoted in W. Bell. 2009. *Foundations of Futures Studies: History, Purposes, and Knowledge.* Vol. 1, (New Jersey: Transaction Publishers), p. 77.

[82] Tufekci, Z. (2014) 'Engineering the Public: Big Data, Surveillance and Computational Politics', First Monday, http://firstmonday.org/ojs/index.php/fm/article/view/4901/4097

[83] B. Monroe, M. Colaresi, and K. Quinn. 2008. Fightin' Words: Lexical Feature Selection and Evaluation for Identifying the Content of Political Conflict. *Political Analysis* 16 (4): 372-403.
[84] Former US Defense Secretary Donald Rumsfeld, February 2002.